MW00623910

Too Cute!

Baby Rabbits

by Christina Leaf

BELLWETHER MEDIA
MINNEAPOLIS, MN

Blastoff! Beginners are developed by literacy experts and educators to meet the needs of early readers. These engaging informational texts support young children as they begin reading about their world. Through simple language and high frequency words paired with crisp, colorful photos, Blastoff! Beginners launch young readers into the universe of independent reading.

Blastoff! Universe

Reading Level — Grade K

Grades 1-3

Grade 4

Sight Words in This Book 🔍

a	in	see
are	is	soon
at	it	the
can	look	their
each	on	they
eat	other	this

This edition first published in 2022 by Bellwether Media, Inc.

Library of Congress Cataloging-in-Publication Data

Names: Leaf, Christina, author.
Title: Baby rabbits / by Christina Leaf.
Description: Minneapolis, MN : Bellwether Media, 2022. | Series: Blastoff! beginners: Too cute! | Includes bibliographical references and index. | Audience: Ages 4-7 | Audience: Grades K-1
Identifiers: LCCN 2021001463 (print) | LCCN 2021001464 (ebook) | ISBN 9781644874899 (library binding) | ISBN 9781648344718 (paperback) | ISBN 9781648343971 (ebook)
Subjects: LCSH: Rabbits--Infancy--Juvenile literature.
Classification: LCC SF453.2 .L427 2022 (print) | LCC SF453.2 (ebook) | DDC 636.932/2--dc23
LC record available at https://lccn.loc.gov/2021001463
LC ebook record available at https://lccn.loc.gov/2021001464

Editor: Amy McDonald   Designer: Jeffrey Kollock

Printed in the United States of America, North Mankato, MN.

313930391121944

Table of Contents

A Baby Rabbit!

Look at the baby rabbit! Hello, kit!

kit

Many kits are
born together.
They are
a **litter**.

litter

Newborn kits
need mom.
They cannot see.

newborn
kits

Kits snuggle
in a nest.
They keep
each other warm.

nest

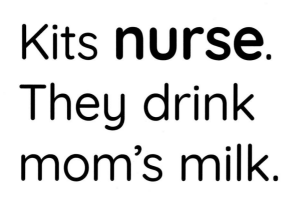

Kits **nurse**.
They drink
mom's milk.

nursing

13

Hopping Around

Kits grow fast!
Soon they
can hop.

Kits keep clean.
They **groom**
their fur.

groom 17

Kits eat plants.
They chew
on grass.

All Grown Up!

This kit is
three weeks old.
It leaves the nest.
Bye, mom!

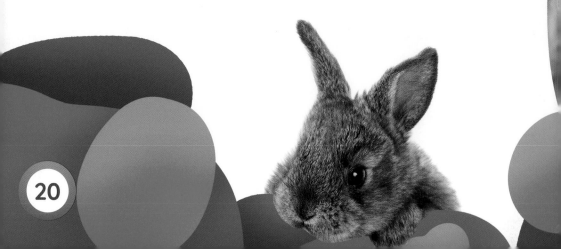

Baby Rabbit Facts

Rabbit Life Stages

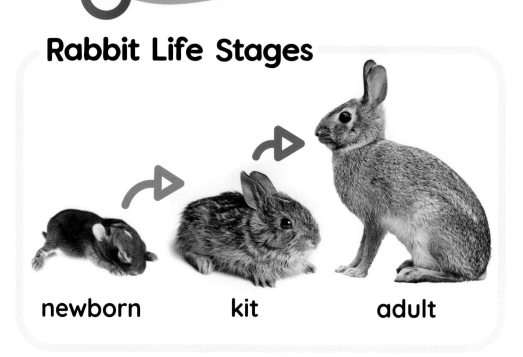

newborn   kit   adult

A Day in the Life

chew grass   groom fur   hop

Glossary

groom

to keep clean

litter

a group of kits born at the same time

newborn

just born

nurse

to drink mom's milk

To Learn More

ON THE WEB

FACTSURFER

Factsurfer.com gives you a safe, fun way to find more information.

1. Go to www.factsurfer.com.

2. Enter "baby rabbits" into the search box and click 🔍.

3. Select your book cover to see a list of related content.

Index